Editor
Eric Migliaccio

Editor in Chief
Ina Massler Levin, M.A.

Creative Director
Karen J. Goldfluss, M.S. Ed.

Illustrator
Renée Mc Elwee

Cover Artist
Brenda DiAntonis

Art Coordinator
Renée Mc Elwee

Imaging
Leonard P. Swierski

Publisher
Mary D. Smith, M.S. Ed.

Grade 4

ANALOGIES for Critical

TCR 3167

D1408251

clock : ticks

cow : moos

A terrific way to:
- Sharpen logical thinking skills
- Prepare for standardized tests
- Understand word relationships
- Improve & develop vocabulary

Teacher Created Resources

Author

Ruth Foster, M.Ed.

Teacher Created Resources
12621 Western Avenue
Garden Grove, CA 92841
www.teachercreated.com

ISBN: 978-1-4206-3167-8

©2011 Teacher Created Resources
Reprinted, 2018
Made in U.S.A.

Teacher Created Resources

Table of Contents

Introduction

Think of an analogy as a wonderful puzzle, and one has a great interdisciplinary teaching exercise.

An analogy is a type of comparison. An analogy is when a likeness is found between two unlike things. If approached as a puzzle, one solves the analogy by finding out how the pieces fit together. What links the words to each other? How can they be connected or tied together? What is the relationship between them?

> **cat** is to **meow** as **dog** is to ___**bark**___

Although the example above may appear to be easy, it is an exercise that involves cognitive processes and critical-thinking skills. One must comprehend the words read, categorize them, understand the connection between them, and then find a similar connection between a different pair of words. In this case, both *meow* and *bark* are sounds that a cat and dog make, respectively.

Analogies written for this series will focus on a variety of word relationships. They will develop, reinforce, and expand skills in the following areas:

→ visual imagery

→ reading comprehension

→ paying attention to detail (word sequence within word pairs)

→ vocabulary development

→ synonym, antonym, and homophone recognition and recall

→ understanding different shades of word meanings

→ reasoning

→ standardized-test taking

Students will be able to demonstrate mastery by doing the following:

→ working with both multiple-choice and write-out question formats

→ analyzing and fixing incorrect analogies

→ writing their own analogies in both question and sentence format

For interdisciplinary practice, some analogies will be subject-specific (addressing science, math, or social studies, for example). Others will push students to think outside of the box, as creative and imaginative connections between words will be asked for. Students may then explain in writing or verbally (depending on skill level) how they created analogous word pairs or situations.

Blank answer sheets can be found on page 60. Use these sheets to provide your students with practice in answering questions in a standardized-test format.

Introducing Analogies

Directions: Fill in the word you think should go in the blank.

1. **Duck** is to **duckling** as **cat** is to _____.

2. **Duck** is to **quack** as **lion** is to _____.

3. **Duck** is to **feathers** as **dog** is to _____.

4. **Duck** is to **wing** as **person** is to _____.

5. **Duck** is to **swim** as **rabbit** is to _____.

What did you just do? You made **analogies**! An analogy is a likeness in some way between things that are otherwise unlike.

A duckling is not a kitten, but a duckling is like a kitten because they are both kinds of animal babies.

Sometimes analogies are written like this:

> **duck : duckling :: cat : kitten**

- The single colon (:) compares two items in a word pair.

- The double colon (::) compares the first word pair to the second word pair.

6. Rewrite question 2, 3, 4, or 5 in the analogy form using colons.

_____   _____   _____   _____

Directions: Fill in the blanks to finish the analogies.

7. male : boy :: female : _____

8. male : father :: female : _____

9. male : uncle :: female : _____

10. male : man :: female : _____

11. male : nephew :: female : _____

12. male : actor :: female : _____

Synonyms in Analogies

A **synonym** is a word that is nearly the **same** in meaning as another word.

1. Which word is *not* a synonym of the others?

   Ⓐ brave   Ⓑ bold   Ⓒ cowardly   Ⓓ fearless

2. Which answer makes the best analogy?

   Ⓐ brave : bold :: cowardly : fearless   Ⓒ cowardly : bold :: brave : fearless

   Ⓑ brave : fearless :: bold : daring   Ⓓ fearless : cowardly :: daring : bold

Directions: Find the synonym that best completes the analogy.

3. **Cry** is to **weep** as **cure** is to _____.

   Ⓐ blubber   Ⓑ sob   Ⓒ hurt   Ⓓ heal

4. **Search** is to **hunt** as **find** is to _____.

   Ⓐ lose   Ⓑ hide   Ⓒ discover   Ⓓ forget

5. **Grin** is to **smile** as **scowl** is to _____.

   Ⓐ frown   Ⓑ chuckle   Ⓒ laugh   Ⓓ giggle

6. **Secret** is to **hidden** as **shatter** is to _____.

   Ⓐ mend   Ⓑ mysterious   Ⓒ open   Ⓓ break

7. **Glance** is to **look** as **glow** is to _____.

   Ⓐ shine   Ⓑ search   Ⓒ see   Ⓓ moon

8. **Travel** is to **move** as **remain** is to _____.

   Ⓐ go   Ⓑ migrate   Ⓒ lift   Ⓓ stay

Directions: Write down four answers. Only one answer should be correct!

9. **Good** is to **excellent** as **bad** is to _____.

   Ⓐ _____   Ⓒ _____

   Ⓑ _____   Ⓓ _____

10. Which one of your answers was correct? Write a sentence telling why. Use the word *synonym* in your sentence.

    _____

    _____

Antonyms in Analogies

An **antonym** is a word that is the **opposite** in meaning of another word.

1. Which word is an antonym of the others?

    Ⓐ elementary   Ⓑ easy   Ⓒ simple   Ⓓ hard

2. What answer makes the best analogy?

    Ⓐ elementary : hard :: dull : exciting   Ⓒ simple : hard :: fast : quick

    Ⓑ hard : easy :: droop : sag   Ⓓ hard : elementary :: beautiful : pretty

---

Directions: Find the antonym that best completes the analogy.

3. **Narrow** is to **wide** as **sorrow** is to _____.

    Ⓐ easy   Ⓑ joy   Ⓒ long   Ⓓ clear

4. **Lower** is to **raise** as **stop** is to _____.

    Ⓐ halt   Ⓑ cease   Ⓒ close   Ⓓ allow

5. **Appear** is to **erase** as **grow** is to _____.

    Ⓐ move   Ⓑ increase   Ⓒ shrink   Ⓓ see

6. **Tear** is to **mend** as **speak** is to _____.

    Ⓐ talk   Ⓑ listen   Ⓒ splash   Ⓓ radio

7. **Expensive** is to **cheap** as **wild** is to _____.

    Ⓐ valuable   Ⓑ crazy   Ⓒ tame   Ⓓ exit

8. **Heartless** is to **kind** as **firm** is to _____.

    Ⓐ wobbly   Ⓑ happy   Ⓒ crazy   Ⓓ nasty

Directions: Write down four answers. Only one answer should be correct!

9. **Lead** is to **follow** as **smooth** is to _____.

    Ⓐ _____   Ⓒ _____

    Ⓑ _____   Ⓓ _____

10. Which one of your answers was correct? Write a sentence telling why. Use the word *antonym* in your sentence.

    _____

    _____

Synonym and Antonym Practice

Directions: Choose the answer that best completes the analogy. Write **synonyms** or **antonyms** on the blank line to describe how the question and answer words are related.

Remember . . .

- Antonyms are words that are opposite in meaning.
- Synonyms are words that mean the same.

---

1. **light : gloom** _____
   - Ⓐ good : nice
   - Ⓑ good : fine
   - Ⓒ good : evil
   - Ⓓ good : proper

2. **gown : dress** _____
   - Ⓐ hat : mitten
   - Ⓑ sock : foot
   - Ⓒ pants : zipper
   - Ⓓ coat : jacket

3. **cheerful : joyful** _____
   - Ⓐ glossy : shiny
   - Ⓑ heavy : light
   - Ⓒ wonderful : awful
   - Ⓓ sick : healthy

4. **throw : catch** _____
   - Ⓐ doze : sleep
   - Ⓑ obey : disobey
   - Ⓒ giggle : laugh
   - Ⓓ tease : pester

5. **release : free** _____
   - Ⓐ hate : love
   - Ⓑ send : receive
   - Ⓒ exit : enter
   - Ⓓ delay : wait

6. **float : sink** _____
   - Ⓐ chew : bite
   - Ⓑ cellar : basement
   - Ⓒ capture : trap
   - Ⓓ doubt : trust

7. **begin : cease** _____
   - Ⓐ create : ruin
   - Ⓑ make : build
   - Ⓒ sketch : draw
   - Ⓓ jump : hop

8. **shiver : quake** _____
   - Ⓐ sing : mumble
   - Ⓑ shove : hug
   - Ⓒ shut : close
   - Ⓓ fight : play

9. **slant : tilt** _____
   - Ⓐ hush : yell
   - Ⓑ mix : shuffle
   - Ⓒ offer : take
   - Ⓓ admire : hate

10. **close : far** _____
    - Ⓐ donate : give
    - Ⓑ mix : separate
    - Ⓒ beg : plead
    - Ⓓ fasten : tie

Synonym and Antonym Analogies

Directions: Write as many synonyms and antonyms as you can think of for the given words. Then, use a thesaurus to add even more words to your list.

		Synonyms	Antonyms
1.	connect		
2.	happy		
3.	wise		
4.	beautiful		
5.	make		

Directions: Write analogy questions using some of the words you wrote down. At least one question should use synonyms and at least one should use antonyms.

6. _____ : _____

Ⓐ_____ : _____

Ⓑ_____ : _____

Ⓒ_____ : _____

Ⓓ_____ : _____

Synonym or antonym: _____   Correct answer: _____

7. _____ : _____

Ⓐ_____ : _____

Ⓑ_____ : _____

Ⓒ_____ : _____

Ⓓ_____ : _____

Synonym or antonym: _____   Correct answer: _____

8. _____ : _____

Ⓐ_____ : _____

Ⓑ_____ : _____

Ⓒ_____ : _____

Ⓓ_____ : _____

Synonym or antonym: _____   Correct answer: _____

Plurals

Directions: Think about how some words are **singular** (one) or **plural** (more than one). Then choose the answer that best completes each analogy. Pay attention to order!

mice : mouse is not the same as mouse : mice

1. mice : mouse is
- (A) singular : plural
- (B) plural : singular

2. mouse : mice is
- (A) singular : plural
- (B) plural : singular

3. fathers : father
- (A) aunt : aunts
- (B) mother : mothers
- (C) woman : women
- (D) babies : baby

4. face : faces
- (A) eye : eyes
- (B) noses : nose
- (C) chins : chin
- (D) lashes : lash

5. cactus : cacti
- (A) horses : horse
- (B) stars : star
- (C) person : people
- (D) boxes : box

6. plates : plate
- (A) cup : cups
- (B) men : man
- (C) spoon : spoons
- (D) wolf : wolves

7. foot : feet
- (A) toes : toe
- (B) leg : legs
- (C) knees : knee
- (D) hands : hand

8. geese : goose
- (A) duck : ducks
- (B) fox : foxes
- (C) oxen : ox
- (D) camel : camels

9. lips : lip
- (A) mouth : mouths
- (B) ear : ears
- (C) cheek : cheeks
- (D) teeth : tooth

10. sheep : sheep
- (A) tree : trees
- (B) tree : leaves
- (C) tree : branch
- (D) tree : oak

11. deer : deer
- (A) child : little
- (B) baby : helpless
- (C) child : children
- (D) baby : cries

12. Write your own analogy using singular and plural words. Make sure only one of your answers is correct!

_____ : _____

(A) _____ : _____   (C) _____ : _____

(B) _____ : _____   (D) _____ : _____

Adjectives

Adjectives are often used in analogies. An adjective is a word that describes a noun. Adjectives answer three questions:

1. What kind is it?   *2.* How many are there?   *3.* Which one is it?

Directions: Fill in the blanks and find the answer that best completes the analogies.

1. In the word pair | **polar bear : white** |, the word __W_____ is an

   __a_____ because it tells what kind of polar bear it is.

2. In the word pair | **ferocious : grizzly bear** |, the word _____ is an

   _____ because it tells what kind of grizzly bear it is.

---

3. **zebra : striped**
   - Ⓐ cheetah : slow
   - Ⓑ giraffe : short
   - Ⓒ eel : slippery
   - Ⓓ bird : furry

4. **sour : lemon**
   - Ⓐ spicy : milk
   - Ⓑ sweet : lime
   - Ⓒ hard : jam
   - Ⓓ hot : pepper

5. **swamp : wet**
   - Ⓐ dry : desert
   - Ⓑ beach : sandy
   - Ⓒ flat : plain
   - Ⓓ rounded : hill

6. **wood : table**
   - Ⓐ toy : stuffed
   - Ⓑ knife : steel
   - Ⓒ bag : plastic
   - Ⓓ rubber : ball

7. **12 : months**
   - Ⓐ 365 : days
   - Ⓑ 365 : years
   - Ⓒ 352 : days
   - Ⓓ 352 : years

8. **dozen : 12**
   - Ⓐ baker's dozen : 11
   - Ⓑ baker's dozen : 12
   - Ⓒ baker's dozen : 13
   - Ⓓ baker's dozen : 14

9. **glue : sticky**
   - Ⓐ desk : soft
   - Ⓑ crayon : colorful
   - Ⓒ board : eraser
   - Ⓓ chair : couch

10. **bright : sun**
   - Ⓐ rain : wet
   - Ⓑ fog : damp
   - Ⓒ frozen : ice
   - Ⓓ snow : white

11. **elephant : huge**
   - Ⓐ fly : large
   - Ⓑ flea : gigantic
   - Ⓒ bee : enormous
   - Ⓓ ant : miniscule

12. Think of three adjectives that might be used to describe each noun.

   • city: _____   _____   _____

   • country: _____   _____   _____

13. Make an analogy using words and answers from question 12.

   _____ : _____ :: _____ : _____

What People Use

Some word pairs in analogies are connected by what people use or need in their jobs.

- **Example:** knight : sword (*person* to *what he/she uses*)

   sword : knight (*what he/she uses* to *person*)

Directions: Choose the answer that best completes each analogy. Then write down other items the person in the question might use.

---

1. **gardener : hoe**
   - Ⓐ pen : writer
   - Ⓑ easel : painter
   - Ⓒ firefighter : hose
   - Ⓓ spacesuit : astronaut

   rake, _____

2. **rope : climber**
   - Ⓐ costume : actor
   - Ⓑ catcher : mitt
   - Ⓒ weaver : loom
   - Ⓓ miner : pick

   _____

3. **jockey : horse**
   - Ⓐ oven : baker
   - Ⓑ plane : pilot
   - Ⓒ ship : captain
   - Ⓓ farmer : tractor

   _____

4. **carpenter : hammer**
   - Ⓐ sink : dishwasher
   - Ⓑ fisherman : net
   - Ⓒ scalpel : surgeon
   - Ⓓ paint : artist

   _____

5. **teacher : chalk**
   - Ⓐ student : child
   - Ⓑ student : learn
   - Ⓒ student : desk
   - Ⓓ student : think

   _____

6. **logger : axe**
   - Ⓐ cook : oven
   - Ⓑ clay : potter
   - Ⓒ brick : mason
   - Ⓓ stone : sculptor

   _____

7. **bloodhound : scent**
   - Ⓐ ladder : firefighter
   - Ⓑ detective : clue
   - Ⓒ shovel : gardener
   - Ⓓ crane : builder

   _____

8. **archer : arrow**
   - Ⓐ runner : race
   - Ⓑ jumper : hop
   - Ⓒ player : win
   - Ⓓ wrestler : mat

   _____

9. **bandage : nurse**
   - Ⓐ nail : hammer
   - Ⓑ mop : janitor
   - Ⓒ key : lock
   - Ⓓ vet : dog

   _____

---

10. Write an analogy using some of the items you wrote on the lines above.

   _____ : _____ :: _____ : _____

Things that Go Together

Directions: Write down what you think of when you read these words:

(There are no wrong answers. Just write down the first thing you think of.)

- pen and _____
- peanut butter and _____
- milk and _____
- bowl and _____
- night and _____

Check to see if the person sitting next to you or other students in your class thought of the same things.

Directions: Choose the answer that best completes the analogies. The connection between the word pairs is *things that go together*.

Hint: Say the bolded words with the word *and* between them (for example, "fish *and* chips").

1. **Fish** is to **chips** as **sugar** is to _____.
   - (A) bag
   - (B) potatoes
   - (C) trout
   - (D) spice

2. **Pillow** is to **bed** as **stamp** is to _____.
   - (A) sheet
   - (B) envelope
   - (C) rest
   - (D) expensive

3. **Bread** is to **butter** as **salt** is to _____.
   - (A) pepper
   - (B) white
   - (C) grainy
   - (D) tasty

4. **Bat** is to **ball** as **bow** is to _____.
   - (A) arrow
   - (B) net
   - (C) sky
   - (D) basket

5. **Table** is to **chair** as **hide** is to _____.
   - (A) smell
   - (B) scream
   - (C) seek
   - (D) sit

6. **Peas** is to **carrots** as **strawberries** is to

   _____.
   - (A) corners
   - (B) cats
   - (C) cream
   - (D) cows

7. **Tooth** is to **nail** as **lock** is to _____.
   - (A) steal
   - (B) key
   - (C) turn
   - (D) code

8. **Pins** is to **needles** as **thunder** is to

   _____
   - (A) cloud
   - (B) frightening
   - (C) flat
   - (D) lightning

Past and Present

A **verb** is an **action** word. A verb tells you what you are doing. Verbs have different tenses.

The **present** tense is for an action that is happening now. The **past** tense is for an action that has already happened.

Directions: Look at the examples of verbs. Write down two more examples using different verbs.

Present		Past	
Today I	sleep	*Yesterday I*	slept
Today I	eat	*Yesterday I*	ate
Today I		*Yesterday I*	
Today I		*Yesterday I*	

Directions: Choose a word from the word box that best completes each analogy.

swung	shut	shook	say	touched
keep	caught	hold	take	rode

1. choose : chose :: catch : _____

2. lock : locked :: touch : _____

3. bent : bend :: kept : _____

4. step : stepped :: swing : _____

5. spent : spend :: held : _____

6. walk : walked :: ride : _____

7. split : split :: shut : _____

8. tore : tear :: took : _____

9. wash : washed :: shake : _____

10. spoke : speak :: said : _____

11. Write down the question numbers of the ones that were . . .

    • present to past _____   • synonyms _____

    • past to present _____   • impossible to tell _____

Where Things Go

Some analogies are based on where things go, where they live, or where they're found.

Directions: Choose the answer that best completes each analogy.

Hint: Pay attention to order: | rug : floor | is not the same as | floor : rug |.

1. **floor : rug** is
   - Ⓐ thing : where goes
   - Ⓑ where goes : thing

2. **rug : floor** is
   - Ⓐ thing : where goes
   - Ⓑ where goes : thing

3. **book : library :: desk :**
   - Ⓐ fire truck
   - Ⓒ computer
   - Ⓑ elevator
   - Ⓓ classroom

4. **whale : ocean :: camel :**
   - Ⓐ desert
   - Ⓒ prairie
   - Ⓑ forest
   - Ⓓ tundra

5. **train : track**
   - Ⓐ boat : ship
   - Ⓒ truck : road
   - Ⓑ plane : flies
   - Ⓓ snow : skis

6. **glass : cupboard**
   - Ⓐ coat : closet
   - Ⓒ wall : picture
   - Ⓑ shelf : book
   - Ⓓ museum : painting

7. **water : penguin**
   - Ⓐ duck : water
   - Ⓒ dolphin : water
   - Ⓑ land : ostrich
   - Ⓓ land : eel

8. **stove : kitchen**
   - Ⓐ paper : pencil
   - Ⓒ oven : cook
   - Ⓑ wall : window
   - Ⓓ dresser : bedroom

9. **student : school**
   - Ⓐ cook : ambulance
   - Ⓒ patient : hospital
   - Ⓑ doctor : pool
   - Ⓓ store : clerk

10. **blanket : bed**
   - Ⓐ sleep : night
   - Ⓒ floor : roof
   - Ⓑ lid : pot
   - Ⓓ sock : shoe

11. Think of two animals that would complete the analogy correctly.

   _____ : ___jungle___ :: _____ : ___city___

Animal Family Names

Directions: Some analogies are based on the names of old, young, male, and female family members. Choose the answer that best completes each analogy.

Hint: Pay attention to order: | **cat : kitten** | is not the same as | **kitten : cat** |.

---

1. **cat : kitten** is

  Ⓐ old : young

  Ⓑ young : old

2. **kitten : cat** is

  Ⓐ old : young

  Ⓑ young : old

---

3. **gander : goose :: male :**

  Ⓐ female   Ⓒ cub

  Ⓑ baby   Ⓓ puppy

4. **stallion : horse :: bull :**

  Ⓐ pup   Ⓒ fawn

  Ⓑ whale   Ⓓ kitten

---

5. **doe : deer**

  Ⓐ male : sheep   Ⓒ lamb : sheep

  Ⓑ ram : sheep   Ⓓ ewe : sheep

6. **cub : fawn**

  Ⓐ seal : pup   Ⓒ duck : cat

  Ⓑ bear : deer   Ⓓ boy : girl

---

7. **bull : calf**

  Ⓐ rooster : hen   Ⓒ stallion : foal

  Ⓑ mare : horse   Ⓓ piglet : boar

8. **drake : duckling**

  Ⓐ peacock : peachick   Ⓒ lamb : ram

  Ⓑ chick : rooster   Ⓓ cub : boar

---

9. **lion : lioness**

  Ⓐ kit : fox   Ⓒ kid : goat

  Ⓑ cub : tiger   Ⓓ rabbit : doe

10. **colt : filly**

  Ⓐ pup : litter   Ⓒ boy : girl

  Ⓑ litter : pup   Ⓓ girl : boy

Directions: Think of animal names that would complete the analogies correctly.

Hints: Any member of the dog family, wild or tame, is a *canine*. Any member of the cat family, wild or tame, is a *feline*.

____canine____ : ____feline____ :: _____ : _____

_____ : ____feline____ :: _____ : ____canine____

Finding the Connection

All of the analogies below have the same connection between the word pairs.

Directions: Choose the answer that best completes each analogy and answer the questions.

Hints:

- First, look at all of the question word pairs. This will help you figure out the big connection.

- Next, watch out for order: | **peel : orange** | is not the same as | **orange : peel** | .

---

1. orange : peel

Ⓐ shell : turtle

Ⓑ turtle : shell

Ⓒ water : turtle

Ⓓ turtle : water

2. crab : shell

Ⓐ deer : buck

Ⓑ buck : deer

Ⓒ deer : hide

Ⓓ hide : deer

3. feather : bird

Ⓐ snake : fur

Ⓑ fur : snake

Ⓒ snake : scale

Ⓓ scale : snake

---

4. scales : fish

Ⓐ shell : snail

Ⓑ tail : snail

Ⓒ foot : snail

Ⓓ head : snail

5. bear : fur

Ⓐ hawk : beak

Ⓑ hawk : leg

Ⓒ hawk : feather

Ⓓ hawk : talon

6. tree : bark

Ⓐ cat : paw

Ⓑ cat : fur

Ⓒ cat : tail

Ⓓ cat : purr

---

7. shell : walnut

Ⓐ otter : fur

Ⓑ peanut : ground

Ⓒ melon : seed

Ⓓ peel : banana

8. person : skin

Ⓐ hide : zebra

Ⓑ wool : sheep

Ⓒ feather : crow

Ⓓ otter : fur

9. cover : book

Ⓐ melon : rind

Ⓑ shell : lobster

Ⓒ pea : pod

Ⓓ horse : donkey

---

10. What is the big connection between the question word pairs?

_____

_____

Finding the Connection 2

Directions: Choose the answer that best completes each analogy and answer the questions.

Hint: Watch out for order: | **boy : foot** | is not the same as | **foot : boy** |.

---

1. **boy : foot**
- Ⓐ dog : tail
- Ⓑ tail : dog
- Ⓒ dog : paw
- Ⓓ paw : dog

2. **girl : arm**
- Ⓐ leaf : tree
- Ⓑ tree : leaf
- Ⓒ branch : tree
- Ⓓ tree : branch

3. **snout : pig**
- Ⓐ trunk : elephant
- Ⓑ elephant : trunk
- Ⓒ man : face
- Ⓓ face : man

4. **tiger : claw**
- Ⓐ dog : paw
- Ⓑ eagle : talon
- Ⓒ horse : hoof
- Ⓓ whale : fin

5. **dolphin : fin**
- Ⓐ monkey : tooth
- Ⓑ monkey : leg
- Ⓒ monkey : nose
- Ⓓ monkey : arm

6. **lung : man**
- Ⓐ fin : fish
- Ⓑ fish : tail
- Ⓒ gill : fish
- Ⓓ fish : scale

7. **boy : girl**
- Ⓐ actor : actress
- Ⓑ actress : actor
- Ⓒ uncle : nephew
- Ⓓ nephew : uncle

8. **woman : man**
- Ⓐ waitress : waiter
- Ⓑ waiter : waitress
- Ⓒ mother : daughter
- Ⓓ daughter : mother

9. **king : queen**
- Ⓐ knight : sir
- Ⓑ sir : knight
- Ⓒ host : hostess
- Ⓓ hostess : host

---

10. What is the big connection in questions 1 through 6? _____

_____

11. What is the big connection in questions 7 through 9? _____

_____

Finding the Connection 3

Directions: Choose the answer that best completes each analogy.

Hint: Watch out for order: | **astronaut : space** | is not the same as | **space : astronaut** | .

1. **astronaut : space**
   - Ⓐ rocket : blast
   - Ⓑ blast : rocket
   - Ⓒ classroom : teacher
   - Ⓓ teacher : classroom

2. **court : judge**
   - Ⓐ lab : scientist
   - Ⓑ scientist : lab
   - Ⓒ glass : drink
   - Ⓓ drink : glass

3. **clerk : store**
   - Ⓐ plane : pilot
   - Ⓑ pilot : plane
   - Ⓒ plane : wing
   - Ⓓ wing : plane

4. **library : librarian**
   - Ⓐ teacher : student
   - Ⓑ student : teacher
   - Ⓒ hospital : doctor
   - Ⓓ doctor : hospital

5. **runner : track**
   - Ⓐ swimmer : pool
   - Ⓑ pool : swimmer
   - Ⓒ swimmer : lap
   - Ⓓ lap : swimmer

6. **field : farmer**
   - Ⓐ weed : garden
   - Ⓑ garden : weed
   - Ⓒ teacher : school
   - Ⓓ school : teacher

7. **bracelet : wrist**
   - Ⓐ neck : necklace
   - Ⓑ necklace : neck
   - Ⓒ coat : winter
   - Ⓓ winter : coat

8. **cook : kitchen**
   - Ⓐ bakery : baker
   - Ⓑ baker : bakery
   - Ⓒ bread : sliced
   - Ⓓ sliced : bread

9. **hand : mitten**
   - Ⓐ scarf : hat
   - Ⓑ hat : scarf
   - Ⓒ sock : foot
   - Ⓓ foot : sock

10. **ship : captain**
    - Ⓐ doctor : nurse
    - Ⓑ nurse : doctor
    - Ⓒ actor : stage
    - Ⓓ stage : actor

11. **reed : marsh**
    - Ⓐ coral : prairie
    - Ⓑ prairie : coral
    - Ⓒ cactus : desert
    - Ⓓ desert : cactus

12. **kite : air**
    - Ⓐ river : canoe
    - Ⓑ canoe : river
    - Ⓒ boat : canoe
    - Ⓓ canoe : boat

13. Describe how, in general, the word pairs in the questions are connected.

_____

Trying Out the Connection

Directions: Write out how the word pairs are connected.

1. **chocolate chip : cookie**

   _C_____ is a kind of _c_____.

2. **sharpen : dull**

   _S_____ is the opposite of _d_____.

3. **hungry : eat**

   If you are _h_____, you _e_____.

Directions: Fill in the words to see what word pair is the correct answer. (**Hint:** There will be only one that makes sense.) Then circle the correct answer.

4. **chocolate chip : cookie**

   Ⓐ worm : robin   Ⓒ penguin : bird

   Ⓑ parrot : colorful   Ⓓ eagle : soars

   - _W_____ is a kind of _r_____.
   - _P_____ is a kind of _c_____.
   - _P_____ is a kind of _b_____.
   - _E_____ is a kind of _s_____.

5. **sharpen : dull**

   Ⓐ snoop : pry   Ⓒ pretend : imagine

   Ⓑ prevent : allow   Ⓓ steal : thief

   - _S_____ is the opposite of _p_____.
   - _P_____ is the opposite of _a_____.
   - _P_____ is the opposite of _i_____.
   - _S_____ is the opposite of _t_____.

6. **hungry : eat**

   Ⓐ wet : swim   Ⓒ happy : weep

   Ⓑ tired : race   Ⓓ thirsty : drink

   - If you are _w_____, you _s_____.
   - If you are _t_____, you _r_____.
   - If you are _h_____, you _w_____.
   - If you are _t_____, you _d_____.

Part to Whole

Some word pairs in analogies are connected by *part to whole* or *whole to part*.

- **Example:** day : week (*part to whole*)

  week : day (*whole to part*)

Directions: Choose the answer that best completes each analogy and answer the questions.

1. **classrooms : school**
- Ⓐ stairs : elevator
- Ⓑ elevators : stairs
- Ⓒ floors : skyscraper
- Ⓓ skyscraper : floors

2. **violin : string**
- Ⓐ piano : key
- Ⓑ key : piano
- Ⓒ drum : beat
- Ⓓ beat : drum

3. **year : month**
- Ⓐ day : light
- Ⓑ minute : second
- Ⓒ week : seven
- Ⓓ summer : hot

4. **page : book**
- Ⓐ cover : protect
- Ⓑ chapter : read
- Ⓒ library : book
- Ⓓ word : sentence

5. **flower : petal**
- Ⓐ banana : yellow
- Ⓑ seed : apple
- Ⓒ orange : section
- Ⓓ melon : soft

6. **block : tower**
- Ⓐ cabin : log
- Ⓑ wall : stone
- Ⓒ fence : wood
- Ⓓ brick : chimney

7. **seasons : summer**
- Ⓐ Monday : days
- Ⓑ months : March
- Ⓒ Tuesday : Thursday
- Ⓓ July : August

8. **play : acts**
- Ⓐ book : chapters
- Ⓑ movie : popcorn
- Ⓒ tent : circus
- Ⓓ fun : work

9. **finger : hand**
- Ⓐ elbow : knee
- Ⓑ toe : foot
- Ⓒ nose : smell
- Ⓓ leg : run

10. **step : staircase**
- Ⓐ elevator : lift
- Ⓑ ladder : rope
- Ⓒ scarf : knit
- Ⓓ letter : alphabet

11. **starfish : arm**
- Ⓐ clam : ocean
- Ⓑ fin : shark
- Ⓒ squid : tentacle
- Ⓓ scale : fish

12. **tree : forest**
- Ⓐ fish : school
- Ⓑ plant : leaf
- Ⓒ grass : cut
- Ⓓ soup : clam

13. List the questions that were

- part to whole: _____1_____, _____

- whole to part: _____

14. Write your own analogy using four of these words or phrases: **table of contents**, **tree**, **legend**, **book**, **rock**, **map**.

_____ : _____ :: _____ : _____

Is your analogy *part to whole* or *whole to part*? _____

Less Than/More Than

Some analogies are based on less than/more than. One word in the word pair might be smaller than, bigger than, or not as strong as the other word.

Directions: Choose the answer that best completes each analogy.

Hint: Pay attention to order: | lake : ocean | is not the same as | ocean : lake | !

---

1. **lake : ocean** is

  Ⓐ less than : more than

  Ⓑ more than : less than

2. **ocean : lake** is

  Ⓐ less than : more than

  Ⓑ more than : less than

---

3. **walk : run**

  Ⓐ cry : sob

  Ⓑ sob : cry

  Ⓒ sing : song

  Ⓓ song : sing

4. **tired : exhausted**

  Ⓐ sleep : bed

  Ⓑ bed : sleep

  Ⓒ hungry : starved

  Ⓓ starved : hungry

5. **drip : pour**

  Ⓐ drink : water

  Ⓑ water : drink

  Ⓒ cut : scratch

  Ⓓ scratch : cut

6. **gallop : trot**

  Ⓐ shout : talk

  Ⓑ talk : shout

  Ⓒ horse : saddle

  Ⓓ saddle : horse

7. **big : gigantic**

  Ⓐ phone : talk

  Ⓑ talk : phone

  Ⓒ cool : freezing

  Ⓓ freezing : cool

8. **race : stroll**

  Ⓐ smell : stink

  Ⓑ stink : smell

  Ⓒ book : school

  Ⓓ school : book

9. **old : ancient**

  Ⓐ baby : dry

  Ⓑ dry : baby

  Ⓒ soaked : wet

  Ⓓ wet : soaked

10. **drizzle : downpour**

  Ⓐ fish : water

  Ⓑ water : fish

  Ⓒ canyon : ditch

  Ⓓ ditch : canyon

11. **look : stare**

  Ⓐ shoe : sock

  Ⓑ sock : shoe

  Ⓒ sip : gulp

  Ⓓ gulp : sip

Directions: Make your own analogies using units of measurement (for example, ounces, inches, kilograms, etc.).

12. _____ : _____ :: _____ : _____

13. _____ : _____ :: _____ : _____

Classifying Analogies

Some analogies are based on how things can be classified, or grouped.

Directions: Fill in the blanks and choose the answer that best completes each analogy.

1. How are purple and black alike?
   - They are both ____c____.

2. How are bananas and apples alike?
   - They are both kinds of ____f____.

Hint: Pay attention to order: | **purple : color** | is not the same as | **color : purple** | !
Purple is always a color. A color is not always purple. So, | **banana : fruit** | is not the same
as | **fruit : banana** |.

3. A ____b____ is always a ____f____.

   A _____ is not always a _____.

---

4. **rose** is to **flower** as
   - Ⓐ dog : Dalmatian
   - Ⓑ Dalmatian : dog

5. **cheetah** is to **feline** as
   - Ⓐ wolf : canine
   - Ⓑ canine : wolf

6. **potato** is to **vegetable** as
   - Ⓐ fruit : banana
   - Ⓑ banana : fruit

7. **furniture** is to **desk** as
   - Ⓐ basketball : game
   - Ⓑ game : basketball

8. **rattlesnake** is to **reptile** as
   - Ⓐ buffalo : mammal
   - Ⓑ mammal : buffalo

9. **tree** is to **pine** as
   - Ⓐ trout : fish
   - Ⓑ fish : trout

10. **bird** is to **parrot** as
    - Ⓐ snake : cobra
    - Ⓑ cobra : snake

11. **muscle** is to **biceps** as
    - Ⓐ cheddar : cheese
    - Ⓑ cheese : cheddar

Classifying Analogies 2

Directions: Fill in the blanks and choose the answer that best completes each analogy.

1. How are a saw and a hammer alike?
   - They are both ____†_____.

2. Why are these word pairs different? | saw : tool | | tool : saw |
   - A ___s_____ is always a _____.
   - A ___†_____ is not always a _____.

---

3. **green : color**
   - Ⓐ fish : minnow
   - Ⓑ fish : salmon
   - Ⓒ fish : trout
   - Ⓓ goldfish : fish

4. **instrument : drum**
   - Ⓐ insect : bee
   - Ⓑ 5 : number
   - Ⓒ May : month
   - Ⓓ monkey : mammal

5. **oak : tree**
   - Ⓐ robin : jay
   - Ⓑ whale : dolphin
   - Ⓒ crow : bird
   - Ⓓ letter : J

6. **flower : tulip**
   - Ⓐ hawk : bird
   - Ⓑ day : Monday
   - Ⓒ 8 : number
   - Ⓓ drill : tool

7. **baseball : game**
   - Ⓐ color : orange
   - Ⓑ carrot : vegetable
   - Ⓒ ball : football
   - Ⓓ animal : horse

8. **shirt : clothes**
   - Ⓐ crocodile : reptile
   - Ⓑ mammal : panther
   - Ⓒ amphibian : frog
   - Ⓓ insect : beetle

9. **fruit : berry**
   - Ⓐ daisy : flower
   - Ⓑ four : number
   - Ⓒ lake : ocean
   - Ⓓ tree : elm

10. **earring : jewelry**
    - Ⓐ star : Sun
    - Ⓑ planet : Saturn
    - Ⓒ Earth : planet
    - Ⓓ planet : Neptune

11. **Mexico : country**
    - Ⓐ country : New York
    - Ⓑ state : California
    - Ⓒ country : Arizona
    - Ⓓ Texas : state

---

12. Write your own answer choices. Make sure only one answer choice is correct.

   | giraffe : mammal |

   - Ⓐ _____ : reptile
   - Ⓑ reptile : _____

13. Tell which answer is correct and why.

   _____

   _____

Practice Making Classes

Directions: Think of the names of as many things as you can that fit in the given classes.

Class	Class Members or Items
1. jobs	teacher,
2. instruments	
3. mammals	
4. reptiles	
5. fruits	
6. dairy foods	

Directions: Write two analogy questions using class names and some of the things you listed as members of each class. One question should have the class first, then an item. One question should have an item first, and then the class.

7. _____ : _____

    Ⓐ _____ : _____

    Ⓑ _____ : _____

    Ⓒ _____ : _____

    Ⓓ _____ : _____

Correct answer: _____

Is your answer *class to member* or *member to class*? _____

8. _____ : _____

    Ⓐ _____ : _____

    Ⓑ _____ : _____

    Ⓒ _____ : _____

    Ⓓ _____ : _____

Correct answer: _____

Is your answer *class to member* or *member to class*? _____

Multiple-Meaning Words

Some words have more than one meaning. For example, the word *drop* can be a noun or a verb.

- A **noun** is a person, place or thing. (There is only one <u>drop</u> left.)
- A **verb** is an action word. (If you <u>drop</u> the glass, it will break.)

Directions: Pick which answer choice best completes each analogy.

1. | The <u>ship</u> sailed. | : | I will <u>ship</u> this box. |

    Ⓐ noun : verb   Ⓑ verb : noun

2. | The <u>fire</u> is hot. | : | <u>Fire</u> anyone who is late! |

    Ⓐ noun : vebrb   Ⓑ verb : noun

3. | We <u>play</u> after school. | : | Seven actors are in the <u>play</u>. |

    Ⓐ noun : verb   Ⓑ verb : noun

4. | Careful! Don't <u>trip</u>! | : | I will take a <u>trip</u> to Spain. |

    Ⓐ noun : verb   Ⓑ verb : noun

5. | The <u>sign</u> says, "Stop." | : | <u>Sign</u> your name here. |

    Ⓐ noun : verb   Ⓑ verb : noun

6. | <u>Watch</u> out for snakes. | : | My <u>watch</u> is on my left wrist. |

    Ⓐ noun : verb   Ⓑ verb : noun

7. | I <u>can</u> swim. | : | Open the <u>can</u> of nuts, please. |

    Ⓐ noun : verb   Ⓑ verb : noun

8. | The <u>show</u> must go on! | : | <u>Show</u> me your paper, please. |

    Ⓐ noun : verb   Ⓑ verb : noun

9. | Don't <u>rock</u> the boat! | : | The <u>rock</u> rolled down the hill. |

    Ⓐ noun : verb   Ⓑ verb : noun

10. | The <u>spy</u> was never caught. | : | What do you <u>spy</u> in the tree? |

    Ⓐ noun : verb   Ⓑ verb : noun

Multiple-Meaning Words 2

Directions: Write out the connection between the word pair in the question. Then choose the answer that best completes each analogy.

Hints: Remember that some words have multiple meanings! Also, watch out for which word comes first in the word pair!

---

1. **ruler : measure**
   - Ⓐ weigh : scale
   - Ⓑ axe : chop
   - Ⓒ king : throne
   - Ⓓ dig : shovel

   You use a ruler to measure.

2. **king : ruler**
   - Ⓐ queen : crown
   - Ⓑ prince : princess
   - Ⓒ mayor : state
   - Ⓓ president : leader

---

3. **light : heavy**
   - Ⓐ start : begin
   - Ⓑ tired : sleepy
   - Ⓒ wide : narrow
   - Ⓓ steal : rob

4. **light : see**
   - Ⓐ oven : bake
   - Ⓑ nail : hammer
   - Ⓒ catch : mitt
   - Ⓓ bulb : glass

---

5. **sun : star**
   - Ⓐ planet : Mars
   - Ⓑ spaceship : moon
   - Ⓒ Earth : planet
   - Ⓓ astronaut : Jupiter

6. **famous : star**
   - Ⓐ known : unknown
   - Ⓑ silly : clown
   - Ⓒ giant : enormous
   - Ⓓ hidden : seen

---

7. **pen : cage**
   - Ⓐ cap : hat
   - Ⓑ kitten : meow
   - Ⓒ flour : flower
   - Ⓓ trap : animal

8. **pen : write**
   - Ⓐ phone : mail
   - Ⓑ box : square
   - Ⓒ house : chimney
   - Ⓓ crayon : color

---

9. Write down two meanings for the word *ring*.

   _____

   _____

10. Make an analogy with the word *ring*.

   _____ : _____ :: _____ : _____

   Which meaning did you use? _____

Math

Directions: Find the answer that best completes each analogy.

1. **67 + 13 : 84 + 16 :: 80 :**

   Ⓐ 80   Ⓑ 90   Ⓒ 100   Ⓓ 110

2. **7 x 8 : 56 :: 5 x 8 :**

   Ⓐ 40   Ⓑ 46   Ⓒ 50   Ⓓ 56

3. **24 – 8 : 44 – 8 :: 16 :**

   Ⓐ 24   Ⓑ 30   Ⓒ 32   Ⓓ 36

4. **odd : even :: 5 :**

   Ⓐ 15   Ⓑ 20   Ⓒ 23   Ⓓ 59

5. **23 + 17 : 40 :: 29 + 11 :**

   Ⓐ 22 + 13   Ⓑ 50 – 26   Ⓒ 80 ÷ 20   Ⓓ 4 x 10

6. **24 ÷ 6 : 4 :: 24 ÷ 4 :**

   Ⓐ 4   Ⓑ 6   Ⓒ 24   Ⓓ 42

7. **100,000 : 1,000,000 :: one hundred thousand :**

   Ⓐ one thousand   Ⓑ ten thousand   Ⓒ one million   Ⓓ ten million

8. **18 : 27 :: 36 :**

   Ⓐ 45   Ⓑ 46   Ⓒ 47   Ⓓ 48

9. $\frac{1}{2} + \frac{1}{2} : \frac{1}{3} + \frac{1}{3} + \frac{1}{3} :: \frac{1}{4} + \frac{1}{4} + \frac{1}{4} + \frac{1}{4} :$

   Ⓐ $\frac{1}{2}$ Ⓑ $\frac{1}{3}$ Ⓒ $\frac{1}{4}$ Ⓓ 1

10. **x : x – 2 :: 10 :**

    Ⓐ 4   Ⓑ 8   Ⓒ 12   Ⓓ 16

Challenge: Write your own analogy using numbers and math symbols.

_____ : _____ :: _____ : _____

Math 2

Directions: Find the answer that best completes each analogy. Use the chart to help you figure out the answers.

uni-	bi-	tri-	quad-	penta-	hex-, sex-	sept-, hept-	oct-	non-	deca-
1	2	3	4	5	6	7	8	9	10

1. **100 years : 10 years :: century : _____**

   Ⓐ decade   Ⓑ pentagon   Ⓒ octuplet   Ⓓ quadrilateral

2. **two-legged : biped :: four-legged : _____**

   Ⓐ triped   Ⓑ pentaped   Ⓒ quadruped   Ⓓ nonped

3. **: ⚙ :: tricycle :**

   Ⓐ nonacycle   Ⓑ heptacycle   Ⓒ bicycle   Ⓓ unicycle

4. **once a year : twice a year :: annual : _____**

   Ⓐ tri-annual   Ⓑ bi-annual   Ⓒ hex-annual   Ⓓ oct-annual

5. ⬠ : ⯃ **:: pentagon : _____**

   Ⓐ hexagon   Ⓑ septagon   Ⓒ octagon   Ⓓ decagon

6. **swim, bike, run : triathlon :: high jump, long jump, hurdles, shot put, 800m run :**

   Ⓐ pentathlon   Ⓑ decathlon   Ⓒ nonathlon   Ⓓ heptathlon

7. **: triplets :: : _____**

   Ⓐ twins   Ⓑ octuplets   Ⓒ sextuplets   Ⓓ quadruplets

8. **square : quadrilateral :: rectangle : _____**

   Ⓐ triangle   Ⓑ quadrilateral   Ⓒ pentagon   Ⓓ hexagon

Think and Write: Long ago, March was the first month of the Roman year. If March was first, what months were most likely the 7th, 8th, 9th, and 10th months? In each month's name, underline the letters that were a clue.

Social Studies

Directions: Find the word that best completes each analogy.

Hint: You may want to use an atlas, a globe, or the Internet to find a more detailed world map.

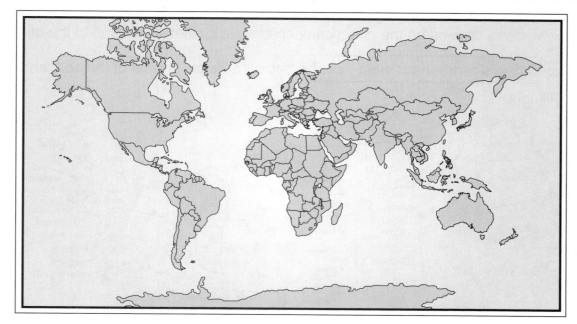

1. Sudan : Africa :: Guatemala : _____

2. USA : North America :: Venezuela : _____

3. Germany : Europe :: India : _____

4. Australia : Australia :: Antarctica : _____

5. Algeria : Argentina :: Africa : _____

6. Indonesia : Switzerland :: Asia : _____

7. Bolivia : Ghana :: South America : _____

8. Kazakhstan : Italy :: Asia : _____

9. Canada : Thailand :: North America : _____

10. South Africa : Southern Hemisphere :: Russia : _____

11. Mexico : Northern Hemisphere:: Uruguay : _____

12. Tanzania : Southern Hemisphere:: Afghanistan : _____

Challenge: Write an analogy using different countries from the ones in the questions.

_____ : _____ :: _____ : _____

Social Studies 2

Directions: Find the state that best completes the analogy. Here are some helpful hints:

- You may want to use a more detailed map of the continental USA.
- Answers will be *north*, *south*, *east*, or *west*.
- Answers will depend on the direction each state is located in relation to the other state.

Example: | Illinois : Indiana :: west : east | because Illinois is west of Indiana, and Indiana is east of Illinois.

1. Alabama : Mississippi :: east : _____

2. Maryland : Virginia :: north : _____

3. Massachusetts : New Hampshire :: south : _____

4. Pennsylvania : New Jersey :: west : _____

5. Florida : Georgia :: south : _____

6. New York : Vermont :: west : _____

7. Kentucky : Tennessee :: north : _____

8. Rhode Island : Connecticut :: east : _____

9. Ohio : West Virginia :: west : _____

10. Indiana : Michigan :: south : _____

Challenge: Write your own analogy using states and directions.

_____ : _____ :: _____ : _____

Science

Directions: Use the chart to help you complete the analogies below.

Name	Field of study
biologist	living things
botanist	plants
geologist	rocks, earth's make-up
herpetologist	reptiles and amphibians
ichthyologist	fishes
meteorologist	atmosphere, weather
paleontologist	fossils
zoologist	animals

1. **dinosaur : paleontologist**
   - (A) frog : geologist
   - (B) cheetah : ichthyologist
   - (C) rock : botanist
   - (D) cloud : meteorologist

2. **zoologist : monkey**
   - (A) biologist : earthquake
   - (B) botanist : cactus
   - (C) geologist : elephant
   - (D) paleontologist : cat

3. **hurricane : meteorologist**
   - (A) lion : herpetologist
   - (B) dolphin : herpetologist
   - (C) lizard : herpetologist
   - (D) tree : herpetologist

4. **geologist : earthquake**
   - (A) ichthyologist : shark
   - (B) fruit tree : botanist
   - (C) tiger : zoologist
   - (D) frog : herpetologist

5. **botanist : flowers**
   - (A) biologist : birds
   - (B) paleontologist : bees
   - (C) ichthyologist : flies
   - (D) geologist : bats

6. **storm : meteorologist**
   - (A) air : zoologist
   - (B) volcano : zoologist
   - (C) corn : zoologist
   - (D) bear : zoologist

7. **cod : ichthyologist**
   - (A) botanist : grass
   - (B) zoologist : wolf
   - (C) volcano : geologist
   - (D) valley : meteorologist

8. **herpetologist : snake**
   - (A) biologist : gold
   - (B) paleontologist : triceratops
   - (C) ichthyologist : cow
   - (D) botanist : crocodile

Think and Write: Would you rather be an entomologist (someone who studies insects) or one of the scientists in the chart above? On a separate piece of paper, write a few sentences explaining your answer.

Spelling

Directions: Use these spelling rules to help you complete the analogies:

- **Rule 1:** Silent *e* helps a vowel say its name. (Think of how *kite* and *kit* sound.)
- **Rule 2:** When two vowels go walking, the first one usually does the talking. (Think of how *wait* is spelled *wait* instead of *wiat*.)

Hint: "Neither Rule" means "does not follow Rule 1 or Rule 2."

---

1. **Mate** is to **Rule 1** as **plate** is to _____.

   Ⓐ Rule 1   Ⓑ Rule 2   Ⓒ Neither Rule

2. **Clean** is to **Rule 2** as **mean** is to _____.

   Ⓐ Rule 1   Ⓑ Rule 2   Ⓒ Neither Rule

3. **Past** is to **Neither Rule** as **paste** is to _____.

   Ⓐ Rule 1   Ⓑ Rule 2   Ⓒ Neither Rule

4. **Rip** is to **Neither Rule** as **ripe** is to _____.

   Ⓐ Rule 1   Ⓑ Rule 2   Ⓒ Neither Rule

5. **Goat** is to **Rule 2** as **got** is to _____.

   Ⓐ Rule 1   Ⓑ Rule 2   Ⓒ Neither Rule

6. **Moon** is to **Neither Rule** as **seed** is to _____.

   Ⓐ Rule 1   Ⓑ Rule 2   Ⓒ Neither Rule

7. **Pile** is to **Rule 1** as **spoon** is to _____.

   Ⓐ Rule 1   Ⓑ Rule 2   Ⓒ Neither Rule

8. **Ran** is to **Neither Rule** as **rain** is to _____.

   Ⓐ Rule 1   Ⓑ Rule 2   Ⓒ Neither Rule

Challenge: Write down an example of your own of a word that fits each of the following:

- Rule 1: _____
- Rule 2: _____
- Neither Rule: _____

Now, make an analogy using two of your words and the rules they follow or don't follow.

_____ : _____ :: _____ : _____

Homophones

Homophones are words that sound alike. Homophones are not spelled the same, and they have different meanings.

Directions: Give three reasons why *grown* and *groan* are homophones.

1. _____

2. _____

3. _____

Directions: Pick the correct homophone from the word box to complete each analogy.

soar	grown	peace	through
sore	groan	piece	threw

1. rope : jumped :: ball : _____

2. night : day :: war : _____

3. unhappy : sad :: ache : _____

4. on top of : over :: by way of : _____

5. water : swim :: air : _____

6. young : little :: old : _____

7. all : whole :: part : _____

8. funny : laugh :: hurts : _____

Question: How do some people remember what the homophones *peace* and *piece* mean? Circle the first three letters in each word to help you find the answer.

peace   **piece**

Answer: They remember that they would like to have a <u>piece</u> of <u>pie</u>!

Directions: Write down what type of pie you would like a piece of. Use the words *piece* and *pie* in your answer.

_____

_____

Homophones 2

Homophones are words that sound alike. Homophones are not spelled the same, and they have different meanings.

Directions: Give three reasons why *flea* and *flee* are homophones.

1. _____

2. _____

3. _____

Directions: Pick the correct homophone from the word box to complete each analogy.

plane	flea	pier	sew
plain	flee	peer	sow

1. appear : vanish :: stay : _____

2. mitt : catch :: needle : _____

3. float : boat :: fly : _____

4. weeds : hoe :: seeds : _____

5. fib : lie :: dock : _____

6. mammal : whale :: insect : _____

7. fancy : decorated :: ordinary : _____

8. repair : fix :: stare : _____

Challenge: Four of the words for the numbers 1–10 have homophones! Can you write out the number words and their homophones?

1	2	3	4	5	6	7	8	9	10

_____   _____

_____   _____

The Seven Wonders

Seven Wonders of the 20th century were chosen by the American Society of Civil Engineers. Civil engineers design and build things such as roads, bridges, or harbors. The Wonders chosen by the engineers scorned the notion "it can't be done."

Directions: Use the information about the Wonders to complete the analogies.

Name	Location	Fun Fact
Channel Tunnel	England/France	beneath English Channel seabed
CN Tower	Toronto, Canada	as heavy as 23,214 large elephants
Empire State Building	New York, USA	tallest building for over 40 years
Golden Gate Bridge	San Francisco, USA	has enough wire to encircle Earth three times
Itaipu Dam	Brazil/Paraguay	largest hydroelectric plant
North Sea Protection Works	Netherlands	keeps sea from flooding below-sea-level country
Panama Canal	Panama	links Atlantic to Pacific Ocean

1. bridge : Golden Gate :: dam : _____

2. canal : Panama :: tunnel : _____

3. Empire State : CN :: Building : _____

4. Canada : Netherlands :: CN Tower : _____

5. over : under :: Golden Gate Bridge : _____

6. New York : San Francisco :: Empire State Building : _____

7. England/France : Brazil/Paraguay :: Channel Tunnel : _____

8. block : link :: North Sea Protection Works : _____

Challenge: Look up one of these Wonders in a book or on the Internet. Write down three more facts.

1. _____

2. _____

3. _____

Amazing Nines

Directions: Use your hands to multiply by nines and complete the analogies below.

Step 1: Put your hands in front of you, palms up, fingers spread.

Step 2: Fold down the finger you are multiplying nine by.
- **Example:** For 9 x 2, fold down the 2nd finger.
  (**Hint:** Thumbs count as fingers, too!)

Step 3: Count the fingers to the left of the folded finger. There is 1. This is the "tens" number.

Step 4: Count the fingers to the right of the folded finger. There are 8. This is the "ones" number.
- **Results:** 1 ten and 8 ones equals 18.   9 x 2 = 18.

1. : 9 x 6
   - (A) 5 tens, 4 ones : 54
   - (B) 4 tens, 5 ones : 45

2. : 9 x 9
   - (A) 1 ten, 8 ones : 18
   - (B) 8 tens, 1 one : 81

3. **6 tens, 3 ones : 63**
   - (A) : 9 x 7
   - (B) : 9 x 7

4. **2 tens, 7 ones : 27**
   - (A) : 9 x 3
   - (B) : 9 x 3

5. **45 : 4 tens, 5 ones**
   - (A) 9 x 5 :
   - (B) 9 x 5 :

6. **72 : 7 tens, 2 ones**
   - (A) 9 x 8 :
   - (B) 9 x 8 :

Fun Down Under

"Down Under" is slang for Australia. Australia is an English-speaking country, but some of its slang, or words used in everyday language, are different from other English-speaking countries. Here is a list of some of those words:

Australian English	American English
barbie	barbecue
biscuit	cookie
bushfire	wild forest fire
nappy	diaper
dummy	baby pacifier
jackaroo/jillaroo	male/female station hand
mate	good friend
outback	interior of Australia
station	large ranch or farm
tomato sauce	ketchup
ute	utility vehicle or pickup truck

Directions: Use the list above to help you find the correct answers. For each analogy, write the Australian English version of the word as your answer.

1. sour : lemon :: sweet : _____

2. male cowboy : female cowboy :: jackaroo : _____

3. truck : ranch :: ute : _____

4. child : pants :: baby : _____

5. enemy : friend :: rival : _____

6. track : train :: road : _____

7. exterior : coastal :: interior : _____

8. bake : oven :: cook : _____

9. What might be one reason Australian station hands were called jackaroos and jillaroos instead of cowboys and cowgirls?

   _____

   _____

10. Why might one want to wash the baby's dummy if it fell on the floor?

   _____

Review of Analogy Types

Directions: Choose the answer that best completes each analogy. Write **synonym**, **antonym**, **plural**, or **adjective** on the blank line to describe how the question and answer words are related. Remember to pay attention to order!

1. **die : dice**
   - (A) toes : toe
   - (B) foot : feet
   - (C) teeth : tooth
   - (D) lips : lip

   _____

2. **calm : peaceful**
   - (A) broken : whole
   - (B) merry : sad
   - (C) right : wrong
   - (D) foolish : silly

   _____

3. **window : glass**
   - (A) banana : apple
   - (B) table : buy
   - (C) chair : wood
   - (D) seed : plant

   _____

4. **harm : protect**
   - (A) lose : find
   - (B) save : keep
   - (C) sip : drink
   - (D) nap : sleep

   _____

5. **major : minor**
   - (A) make : create
   - (B) hidden : secret
   - (C) begin : start
   - (D) different : same

   _____

6. **stroke : pet**
   - (A) rude : polite
   - (B) talk : speak
   - (C) egg : white
   - (D) edge : center

   _____

7. **green : grass**
   - (A) sour : lime
   - (B) lemon : eat
   - (C) red : blue
   - (D) pen : pencil

   _____

8. **houses : house**
   - (A) mice : mouse
   - (B) step : steps
   - (C) ladder : ladders
   - (D) room : rooms

   _____

9. **present : gift**
   - (A) pot : cook
   - (B) spoon : fork
   - (C) trail : path
   - (D) bonnet : girl

   _____

10. **coat : warm**
    - (A) scarf : mitten
    - (B) scarf : sock
    - (C) scarf : neck
    - (D) scarf : blue

    _____

11. **arrive : leave**
    - (A) fool : trick
    - (B) build : destroy
    - (C) look : glance
    - (D) nap : sleep

    _____

12. **page : pages**
    - (A) pins : pins
    - (B) pens : pens
    - (C) pants : pants
    - (D) purses : purses

    _____

13. Why is question 12 tricky? _____

Review of Analogy Types 2

Directions: Choose the answer that best completes the analogies. Write **homophone**, **purpose**, **member to group**, **past/present**, **male/female**, or **less than/more than** on the blank line to describe how the question and answer words are related. Use each type exactly two times. Remember to pay attention to order!

1. **duke : duchess**
- Ⓐ king : castle
- Ⓑ castle : king
- Ⓒ king : queen
- Ⓓ queen : king

_____

2. **telescope : look**
- Ⓐ needle : sew
- Ⓑ tree : cut
- Ⓒ plant : dress
- Ⓓ house : room

_____

3. **puddle : lake**
- Ⓐ cake : slice
- Ⓑ city : town
- Ⓒ ocean : pond
- Ⓓ hut : castle

_____

4. **toad : towed**
- Ⓐ frog : croak
- Ⓑ flu : flew
- Ⓒ pond : push
- Ⓓ hop : barge

_____

5. **princess : prince**
- Ⓐ lady : lord
- Ⓑ actor : actress
- Ⓒ nephew : niece
- Ⓓ sir : madam

_____

6. **dug : dig**
- Ⓐ creep : crept
- Ⓑ see : saw
- Ⓒ bought : buy
- Ⓓ freeze : froze

_____

7. **ant : insect**
- Ⓐ ape : gorilla
- Ⓑ gorilla : ape
- Ⓒ fish : swim
- Ⓓ swim : fish

_____

8. **nudge : shove**
- Ⓐ drink : water
- Ⓑ talk : shout
- Ⓒ swim : play
- Ⓓ jump : run

_____

9. **spin : spun**
- Ⓐ chose : choose
- Ⓑ lost : lose
- Ⓒ kept : keep
- Ⓓ shoot : shot

_____

10. **vegetable : pea**
- Ⓐ tree : redwood
- Ⓑ pansy : flower
- Ⓒ pear : fruit
- Ⓓ soccer : game

_____

11. **made : maid**
- Ⓐ mat : rug
- Ⓑ glass : cup
- Ⓒ deer : dear
- Ⓓ ring : finger

_____

12. **call : telephone**
- Ⓐ movie : watch
- Ⓑ sponge : wipe
- Ⓒ book : read
- Ⓓ listen : radio

_____

13. If the wrong answers for question 12 had been written in a different order, would they have been correct?

_____

Use What You Know

Sometimes you may not know a word. Don't give up! Sometimes you can figure out the answer by using what you know.

Directions: Go through the answer choices. On the lines to the right, write down how the words you know are connected. Cross out the ones that do not have the same connection as the words in the question. The correct answer will be the one that is not crossed out.

How Words Are Connected

1. **wonderful : horrible**   antonyms
   Ⓐ cow : calf   not antonyms; calf is a baby cow
   Ⓑ enormous : huge
   Ⓒ garrulous : silent   ?????
   Ⓓ hat : head

2. **Most likely, if one is *garrulous*, one**
   Ⓐ doesn't speak.   Ⓒ stays still.   Ⓑ is talkative.   Ⓓ moves around a lot.

How Words Are Connected

3. **giggling : laughing**
   Ⓐ petrified : still   ?????
   Ⓑ house : door
   Ⓒ fly : bird
   Ⓓ standing : sitting

4. **Most likely, when one is *petrified*, one is**
   Ⓐ standing   Ⓒ moving.   Ⓑ not standing   Ⓓ not moving.

5. Look up the words *garrulous* and *petrified* in the dictionary. Write down what they mean.
   • garrulous: _____
   • petrified: _____

Next, rewrite the following sentences on the back of this paper, but substitute <u>garrulous</u> or <u>petrified</u> for the underlined words.

   • My sister is so <u>talkative</u> that she doesn't know what a one-word answer is!
   • At first I was <u>unable to move</u> at the thought of skydiving, but now it's fun.

Now, use the words *garrulous* and *petrified* in two sentences of your own.

_____

_____

Use What You Know 2

Sometimes you may not know a word. Don't give up! Sometimes you can figure out the answer by using what you know.

Directions: Go through the answer choices. On the lines to the right, write down how the words you know are connected. Cross out the ones that do not have the same connection as the words in the question. The correct answer will be the one that is not crossed out.

How Words Are Connected

1. **fawn : deer**
- (A) rooster : hen
- (B) cow : bull
- (C) duck : duckling
- (D) cygnet : swan

_____
_____
_____
_____
_____

2. **Most likely, a *cygnet* is a**
- (A) baby swan.
- (C) female swan.
- (B) male swan.
- (D) group of swans.

How Words Are Connected

3. **herd : cattle**
- (A) troop : baboon
- (B) sheep : flock
- (C) puppy : dog
- (D) mare : horse

_____
_____
_____
_____

4. **Most likely, a *troop* is a**
- (A) male baboon.
- (C) group of baboons.
- (B) baby baboon.
- (D) female baboon.

5. **stallion : horse**
- (A) cub : bear
- (B) drone : bee
- (C) sheep : ewe
- (D) fox : vixen

6. **dog : pack**
- (A) horse : foal
- (B) duckling : duck
- (C) rhinoceros : crash
- (D) herd : deer

7. **Most likely, a *drone* is a**
- (A) male bee.
- (B) female bee.
- (C) baby bee.
- (D) group of bees.

8. **Most likely, a *crash* is a**
- (A) male rhinoceros.
- (B) baby rhinoceros.
- (C) female rhinoceros.
- (D) group of rhinoceros.

Challenge: Find other animal and group names using books or the Internet (key search words: *animal names*, *animal group names*). Write your own analogy using some of the names.

_____ : _____ :: _____ : _____

Analogies in Writing

Directions: First, think of an owl. Then, think of a person. Write down two ways a person might be thought to be like an owl.

1. _____

2. _____

An analogy is a likeness in some ways between things that are otherwise unlike. Writers often use analogies. They use them to help readers make pictures in their heads.

Directions: For #1–4, choose the answer that best completes this sentence:

If a writer compares a person to an owl, the writer may want the reader to make a picture in his or her head of a . . .

1. Ⓐ wise person.   Ⓑ foolish person.

2. Ⓐ person who is *diurnal* (most active during the day).

   Ⓑ person who is *nocturnal* (most active during the night).

3. Ⓐ person who speaks quickly and mumbles nonsense.

   Ⓑ person who speaks slowly and expresses good ideas.

4. Ⓐ person who sometimes likes to be alone.

   Ⓑ person who always has to be in the center of a merry group.

5. Fill in the blanks with an appropriate animal name (except owl) to complete the analogy.

   • diurnal : _____ :: nocturnal : _____

Challenge: Make an analogy where you compare yourself, a person from history, or a person from a book (real or make-believe) to an animal. Explain your comparison below.

_____ : _____
(person)   *(animal)*

_____ is/am a _____

because _____

_____

_____

Analogies in Writing 2

Remember that an **analogy** is a likeness in some way between things that are otherwise unlike.

Directions: Complete the sentence and write more sentences to finish the analogies. Make sure you use lots of descriptive words to help the reader make a picture in his or her head.

1. I know someone who is like the sun because

    _____

    _____

    _____

    _____

2. A book is like a good friend because

    _____

    _____

    _____

    _____

3. When I looked at the puppies, I felt as if I were at a three-ring circus because

    _____

    _____

    _____

    _____

4. The desert is like another planet because

    _____

    _____

    _____

    _____

Now, share one of your analogies with the class.

Far Out Analogies

Directions: Think outside the box! Make up analogies that are so far out that they are silly. Have fun and be creative!

- **Example 1:** beetles : mouth :: elephants : room
- **Link:** You don't want beetles in your mouth, just like you don't want elephants in your room!
- **Example 2:** red : teeth :: purple : knees
- **Link:** Red teeth are as bad or as strange as purple knees are bad or strange!

1. **slug : shoe :: spider :** _____
   - **Link:** _____
   _____

2. **moon : bike :: Mars :** _____
   - **Link:** _____
   _____

3. **paint : honey :: carve :** _____
   - **Link:** _____
   _____

4. **cement : eat ::** _____ : _____
   - **Link:** _____
   _____

5. **nose : see ::** _____ : _____
   - **Link:** _____
   _____

6. _____ : _____ **as** _____ : _____
   - **Link:** _____
   _____

7. _____ : _____ **as** _____ : _____
   - **Link:** _____
   _____

Read one of your analogies to your classmates. Could anyone figure out the link?

Analogies in Reading

Directions: Read the passage. Answer the questions below.

Mrs. Shing said, "Class, Robert Scott's journal was just found in Antarctica. Scott was a famous British explorer. He was in a race to be the first person to reach the South Pole. Scott reached the pole on January 17, 1912, only to find he had come in second. Roald Amundsen from Norway had gotten there first on December 14, 1911. Scott never made it back. He and all his men died from hunger, cold, and exhaustion."

Mrs. Shing continued, "The man who found the journal is going to sell it. The price will be high. This is because the journal will give new details about what really happened. One entry is about a polar bear attack. No one knew about the attack before. Everyone will want to read about it."

Landon said, "Something about that journal isn't right. I'm in the dark, bumping into things, completely lost. Still, I'm going to try and find my way until I see the light."

Suddenly, Raina cried, "A light bulb just went off in my head, and I can see! Landon is right that something is wrong! The journal is a fake because polar bears don't live in Antarctica! They only live in the Arctic, up near the North Pole."

---

1. In the story, the phrase "being in the dark" is an analogy for

   Ⓐ understanding.

   Ⓑ not understanding.

2. In the story, "a light bulb going off" is an analogy for

   Ⓐ getting an idea.

   Ⓑ not getting an idea.

3. Explain why the phrases "being in the dark" and "a light bulb going off" help the reader picture how Landon and Raina feel in the story.

   _____

   _____

   _____

   _____

Challenge: Look in books or on the Internet to find and read parts of Scott's real journal.

Analogies in Reading 2

Directions: Read the passage. Answer the questions below.

"I know about a race that isn't a race," Cory said. "It's an invitation to being cooked alive."

"How can you compare a race to being cooked alive?" asked Nora.

"When it's the Badwater Ultramarathon," Cory answered. "The race begins in Death Valley, California. It goes for 135 miles. Runners have just six days to finish. The race takes place in July. Temperatures sizzle. Air temperature is often 130 degrees F (54°C), but the road can heat up to 200 degrees F (93°C). Runners have to run on the road's white lines. If they don't, their track shoes will melt."

"No one can survive that!" Nora exclaimed.

"Most super athletes can't," Cory said, "but in 2007, Valmir Nunez from Brazil finished in less than 23 hours!"

"So you could say Nunez really cooked," laughed Nora.

"Yes," said Cory. "He burned the competition."

---

1. Most likely Cory makes an analogy between the race and being cooked alive because

   Ⓐ the race is in an oven.

   Ⓑ the race is in a place that is as hot as an oven.

2. When Nora said that "Nunez really cooked," she mainly meant that

   Ⓐ Nunez ran at a very fast speed.

   Ⓑ Nunez got really hot when he ran.

3. Explain how comparing the race to "an invitation to being cooked alive" helps a reader picture how it is to run in the Badwater Ultramarathon.

   _____

   _____

   _____

   _____

   _____

Challenge: Find out how you can enter the Badwater Ultramarathon by looking in books or on the Internet.

Analogies in Reading 3

Directions: Read the passage. Answer the questions below.

"I've brought the world to the table," Ben's father said.

"What do you mean?" asked Ben.

"We have potatoes. Potatoes first came from South America. We're having corn. Corn came from Central America. And we're having blueberries from North America, as well as kiwi fruit from Asia."

"That's surprising," said Hana, Ben's sister. "I thought kiwi fruit came from New Zealand. After all, people from New Zealand are known as 'kiwis.'"

"That's right," Ben's mother said. "Today, kiwi fruit is grown in New Zealand. It's exported around the world, but the fruit's origins, or beginnings, were in Asia."

Ben's father added, "We have macadamia nuts and walnuts. Macadamia nuts originated in Australia. Walnuts were first grown in Europe."

"Is there anything from Africa?" asked Ben.

"Coffee for the adults," laughed Ben's father and mother.

---

1. Ben's father said that he "brought the world to the table" because

    Ⓐ he brought a world map or globe to the table.

    Ⓑ he was making an analogy about the foods' origins.

2. From the story, you can tell that kiwi fruit

    Ⓐ wasn't always exported from New Zealand.

    Ⓑ has always been known as kiwi fruit.

3. Complete the analogy below. Follow these rules:

    • In the first blank, write your name or place you are from.

    • In the second blank, write your personal, state, or country nickname.

    > New Zealand : kiwis :: _____ : _____

Challenge: Look in books or on the Internet to find out the origins of some other foods, such as bananas, watermelons, tomatoes, tea, and chickens.

Connection Review

Directions: Look at the word pairs in the first column. Think about how they are connected. Match the word pairs in the first column with a phrase from the second column that tells how they are connected. The first one has been done for you.

Hints: Use each phrase only once. If you do not know an answer right away, skip it. Come back to it at the end.

Word Pairs	How They Are Connected
_____ J _____ 1. **barn** to **farm**	**A.** antonym (opposite)
_____ 2. **weight** to **wait**	**B.** synonym (same meaning)
_____ 3. **thought** to **think**	**C.** homophone (same sound)
_____ 4. **ferocious** to **gentle**	**D.** multiple-meaning word
_____ 5. **fire truck** to **red**	**E.** adjective
_____ 6. **ewe : lamb**	**F.** classifying (group to member)
_____ 7. **leaf : leaves**	**G.** past to present
_____ 8. **box : carton**	**H.** one to more (plural)
_____ 9. **salt : pepper**	**I.** purpose
_____ 10. **can : can**	**J.** where things go
_____ 11. **scale : weigh**	**K.** things or words that go together
_____ 12. **dog : Dalmatian**	**L.** family names

Challenge: Write two sentences. In each sentence, use the multiple-meaning word from above in a different way.

1. _____

_____

2. _____

_____

Connection Review 2

Directions: Look at the word pairs in the first column. Think about how they are connected. Match the word pairs in the first column with a phrase from the second column that tells how they are connected. The first one has been done for you.

Hints: Use each phrase only once. If you do not know an answer right away, skip it. Come back to it at the end.

Word Pairs	How They Are Connected
_K_ 1. **skyscraper** to **tall**	**A.** antonym (opposite)
_____ 2. **storm : hurricane**	**B.** synonym (same meaning)
_____ 3. **park** to **park**	**C.** homophone (same sound)
_____ 4. **disturb** to **annoy**	**D.** less than/more than
_____ 5. **artist** to **paintbrush**	**E.** family names
_____ 6. **remember** to **forget**	**F.** what people use
_____ 7. **penguin : feathers**	**G.** part name to animal
_____ 8. **knew** to **new**	**H.** multiple-meaning word
_____ 9. **actor** to **actress**	**I.** outside or on top
_____ 10. **mare** to **colt**	**J.** classifying (member to group)
_____ 11. **bench : furniture**	**K.** adjective
_____ 12. **paw : lion**	**L.** male to female

Challenge: Write two sentences. In each sentence, use the multiple-meaning word from above in a different way.

1. _____

   _____

2. _____

   _____

Practice Being the Teacher

Directions: It is your turn to teach. Look at the word pair in the box. Show how to find the answer to the analogy.

| approach : near |

- Ⓐ appear : disappear
- Ⓑ reptile : eggs
- Ⓒ practice : rehearse
- Ⓓ shrink : grow

1. First, write out how the words in the box are connected.

   - If you a_____ something, you n_____ it.

   Next, try out the connection with the other word pairs.

   - If you a_____ something, you d_____ it.

   - If you r_____ something, you e_____ it.

   - If you p_____ something, you r_____ it.

   - If you s_____ something, you g_____ it.

2. Answers _____ and _____ cannot be right because they have the same connection.
   They are both _____. (*synonyms* or *antonyms*)

3. Answer _____ cannot be right because the words in the word pair are not
   _____. (*synonyms* or *antonyms*)

---

4. Which would be the answer if the question were | **teach : taught** | ?

   - Ⓐ slept : sleep
   - Ⓑ heard : hear
   - Ⓒ learn : students
   - Ⓓ weigh : weighed

5. Answers _____ and _____ are wrong because the verb tense is written in the wrong
   order. It should be ___present___ to _____, not _____
   to _____.

6. Answer _____ is wrong because the words are not connected in the same way. The
   word _____ is not the past tense of _____.

Practice Being the Teacher 2

Directions: It is your turn to teach. Look at the word pair in the box. Show how to find the answer to the analogy.

> **map : locate**

- Ⓐ donate : give
- Ⓑ grab : tweezers
- Ⓒ shame : embarrass
- Ⓓ screwdriver : turn

1. Write out how the words in the box are connected.

   Ⓐ You use a d_____ to g_____ .

   Ⓑ You use a g_____ to t_____ .

   Ⓒ You use a s_____ to e_____ .

   Ⓓ You use a s_____ to t_____ .

2. Answers _____ and _____ cannot be right because they have the same connection. They are both _____. (*synonyms* or *antonyms*)

3. Answer _____ cannot be right because it is in the wrong order.

---

4. Which would be the answer if the question were | **whale : mammal** | ?

   - Ⓐ amphibian : newt
   - Ⓑ frogs : amphibians
   - Ⓒ crocodile : reptile
   - Ⓓ mammal : dolphin

5. Answer _____ is wrong because the first word is plural (more than one).

6. Answers _____ and _____ are wrong because they are written in the wrong order.

7. Write your own analogy question with answers. Explain how to solve your analogy to a classmate.

   _____ : _____ :: _____ : _____

   Ⓐ _____ : _____   Ⓒ _____ : _____

   Ⓑ _____ : _____   Ⓓ _____ : _____

Practice What You Know

Directions: Find the answer that best completes each analogy. Remember to . . .

- pay attention to word order
- think about how the words are connected
- read every answer choice
- cross out the ones that can't be right.

---

1. **fiction : fact**
   - (A) easy : simple
   - (B) cruel : kind
   - (C) smooth : even
   - (D) gloomy : sad

2. **bird : chirp**
   - (A) roar : lion
   - (B) honk : goose
   - (C) horse : neigh
   - (D) grunt : pig

3. **boat : row**
   - (A) canoe : paddle
   - (B) fly : plane
   - (C) drive : car
   - (D) pedal : bike

4. **shy : timid**
   - (A) parched : wet
   - (B) young : old
   - (C) active : lazy
   - (D) tidy : clean

5. **boot : shoe**
   - (A) rope : jump
   - (B) kick : ball
   - (C) diamond : gem
   - (D) sock : knee

6. **drawer : chest**
   - (A) word : letter
   - (B) book : chapter
   - (C) chapter : letter
   - (D) shelf : bookcase

7. **hare : hair**
   - (A) meet : meat
   - (B) feet : fat
   - (C) care : cart
   - (D) pair : pant

8. **forgive : forgave**
   - (A) ate : eat
   - (B) leave : left
   - (C) shook : shake
   - (D) wound : wind

9. **pride : lions**
   - (A) birds : flock
   - (B) pack : wolves
   - (C) bees : swarm
   - (D) elephants : herd

10. **python : snake**
    - (A) hole : gopher
    - (B) garden : mole
    - (C) mouse : tail
    - (D) rat : rodent

11. **breeze : tornado**
    - (A) breathe : pant
    - (B) leg : shin
    - (C) tree : bark
    - (D) sweat : hot

12. **present : bow**
    - (A) drink : glass
    - (B) stir : bowl
    - (C) jar : label
    - (D) wrap : open

Challenge: Make an analogy with your state and capital where you live. Use other state and city names for answer choices. Only one answer should be correct.

_____ : _____

(your state)   *(your capital)*

(A) _____ : _____   (C) _____ : _____

(B) _____ : _____   (D) _____ : _____

Practice What You Know 2

Directions: Find the answer that best completes each analogy. Remember to . . .

- pay attention to word order
- think about how the words are connected
- read every answer choice
- cross out the ones that can't be right.

---

1. rose : thorn
- (A) cactus : desert
- (B) desert : cactus
- (C) cactus : spine
- (D) spine : cactus

2. bat : wing
- (A) boy : ball
- (B) plane : fly
- (C) dish : plate
- (D) girl : arm

3. frog : tadpole
- (A) bird : egg
- (B) dog : puppy
- (C) kitten : cat
- (D) cub : bear

4. ring : finger
- (A) blanket : bed
- (B) dish : break
- (C) apple : fruit
- (D) necklace : bead

5. alarm : calm
- (A) open : unwrap
- (B) smile : grin
- (C) glance : see
- (D) spend : save

6. comb : teeth
- (A) table : legs
- (B) chair : sit
- (C) lamp : floor
- (D) sink : kitchen

7. hide : hid
- (A) broke : break
- (B) blow : blew
- (C) bit : bite
- (D) bent : bend

8. giraffe : spotted
- (A) grey : wolf
- (B) badger : digs
- (C) skunk : striped
- (D) sheep : grazes

9. pitch : throw
- (A) eat : food
- (B) exit : enter
- (C) study : examine
- (D) swim : climb

10. clock : ticks
- (A) cow : moos
- (B) cow : grazes
- (C) cow : calf
- (D) cow : milk

11. pie : crust
- (A) apple : red
- (B) taco : shell
- (C) cookie : tasty
- (D) bean : plant

12. fir : tree
- (A) net : catch
- (B) rod : reel
- (C) elm : oak
- (D) salmon : fish

Challenge: Make answer choices for the word pair in the box. Make sure only one answer choice is correct.

> **dim : bright**

(A) _____ : _____   (C) _____ : _____

(B) _____ : _____   (D) _____ : _____

Answer Sheets

These sheets may be used to provide practice in answering questions in a standardized-test format.

Student's Name: _____

_____

Activity Page: _____

1. Ⓐ   Ⓑ   Ⓒ   Ⓓ

2. Ⓐ   Ⓑ   Ⓒ   Ⓓ

3. Ⓐ   Ⓑ   Ⓒ   Ⓓ

4. Ⓐ   Ⓑ   Ⓒ   Ⓓ

5. Ⓐ   Ⓑ   Ⓒ   Ⓓ

6. Ⓐ   Ⓑ   Ⓒ   Ⓓ

7. Ⓐ   Ⓑ   Ⓒ   Ⓓ

8. Ⓐ   Ⓑ   Ⓒ   Ⓓ

9. Ⓐ   Ⓑ   Ⓒ   Ⓓ

10. Ⓐ   Ⓑ   Ⓒ   Ⓓ

11. Ⓐ   Ⓑ   Ⓒ   Ⓓ

12. Ⓐ   Ⓑ   Ⓒ   Ⓓ

Student's Name: _____

_____

Activity Page: _____

1. Ⓐ   Ⓑ   Ⓒ   Ⓓ

2. Ⓐ   Ⓑ   Ⓒ   Ⓓ

3. Ⓐ   Ⓑ   Ⓒ   Ⓓ

4. Ⓐ   Ⓑ   Ⓒ   Ⓓ

5. Ⓐ   Ⓑ   Ⓒ   Ⓓ

6. Ⓐ   Ⓑ   Ⓒ   Ⓓ

7. Ⓐ   Ⓑ   Ⓒ   Ⓓ

8. Ⓐ   Ⓑ   Ⓒ   Ⓓ

9. Ⓐ   Ⓑ   Ⓒ   Ⓓ

10. Ⓐ   Ⓑ   Ⓒ   Ⓓ

11. Ⓐ   Ⓑ   Ⓒ   Ⓓ

12. Ⓐ   Ⓑ   Ⓒ   Ⓓ

Answer Key

Introducing Analogies (page 4)
1. kitten
2. roar
3. fur
4. arm or hand
5. hop or jump
6. Check answers for accuracy.
7. girl
8. mother
9. aunt
10. woman
11. niece
12. actress

Synonyms in Analogies (page 5)
1. C	5. A
2. B	6. D
3. D	7. A
4. C	8. D

Antonyms in Analogies (page 6)
1. D	5. C
2. A	6. B
3. B	7. C
4. D	8. A

Synonym and Antonym Practice (page 7)
1. C, antonyms
2. D, synonyms
3. A, synonyms
4. B, antonyms
5. D, synonyms
6. D, antonyms
7. A, antonyms
8. C, synonyms
9. B, synonyms
10. B, antonyms

Synonym and Antonym Analogies (page 8)
Accept appropriate responses.

Plurals (page 9)
1. B	7. B
2. A	8. C
3. D	9. D
4. A	10. A
5. C	11. C
6. B	

Adjectives (page 10)
1. white, adjective
2. ferocious, adjective
3. C
4. D
5. B
6. D
7. A
8. C
9. B
10. C
11. D
12. Accept appropriate responses.

What People Use (page 11)
1. C	6. A
2. A	7. B
3. D	8. D
4. B	9. B
5. C	

Things that Go Together (page 12)
1. D	5. C
2. B	6. C
3. A	7. B
4. A	8. D

Past and Present (page 13)
1. caught
2. touched
3. keep
4. swung
5. hold
6. rode
7. shut
8. take
9. shook
10. say
11. present to past: 1, 2, 4, 6, 9; past to present: 3, 5, 8, 10; impossible to tell: 7; synonyms: 10

Past and Present 2 (page 14)
1. A	5. D
2. B	6. D
3. C	7. B
4. B	8. A

Purpose (page 15)
1. A
2. B
3. D
4. A
5. C
6. C
7. B
8. D
9. B
10. A
11. B (phone : call); C (broom : sweep); D (alarm : warn)
12. Accept appropriate responses.

Where Things Go (page 16)
1. B	6. A
2. A	7. B
3. D	8. D
4. A	9. C
5. C	10. B

Animal Family Names (page 17)
1. A	6. B
2. B	7. C
3. A	8. A
4. B	9. D
5. D	10. C

Finding the Connection (page 18)
1. B
2. C
3. D
4. A
5. C
6. B
7. D
8. D
9. B
10. The big connection has something to do with what is on the outside or covering something.

Answer Key *(cont.)*

Finding the Connection 2 (page 19)
1. C
2. D
3. A
4. B
5. D
6. C
7. A
8. A
9. C
10. whole to part, or part to whole
11. male to female, or female to male

Finding the Connection 3 (page 20)
1. D
2. A
3. B
4. C
5. A
6. D
7. B
8. B
9. D
10. D
11. C
12. B
13. where things go, belong, work, or are found

Trying Out the Connection (page 21)
1. Chocolate chip is a kind of cookie.
2. Sharpen is the opposite of dull.
3. If you are hungry, you eat.
4. C
5. B
6. D

Part to Whole (page 22)
1. C
2. A
3. B
4. D
5. C
6. D
7. B
8. A
9. B
10. D
11. C
12. A
13. part to whole: 1, 4, 6, 9, 10, 12; whole to part: 2, 3, 5, 7, 8, 11
14. (order may vary) table of contents : book :: legend : map

Less Than/More Than (page 23)
1. A
2. B
3. A
4. C
5. D
6. A
7. C
8. B
9. D
10. D
11. C

Classifying Analogies (page 24)
1. colors
2. fruit
3. A banana is always a fruit; a fruit is not always a banana.
4. B
5. A
6. B
7. B
8. A
9. B
10. A
11. B

Classifying Analogies 2 (page 25)
1. tools
2. A saw is always a tool; a tool is not always a saw.
3. D
4. A
5. C
6. B
7. B
8. A
9. D
10. C
11. D
12. A
13. Accept appropriate responses.

Practice Making Classes (page 26)
Accept appropriate responses.

Multiple-Meaning Words (page 27)
1. A
2. A
3. B
4. B
5. A
6. B
7. B
8. A
9. B
10. A

Multiple-Meaning Words 2 (page 28)
1. B
2. D, A king is a ruler.
3. C, antonyms, or something light is not heavy.
4. A, You use a light to see.
5. C, The sun is a star.
6. B, A star (person) is famous.
7. A, A pen is a type of cage.
8. D, You use a pen to write.
9. Accept appropriate responses.
10. Accept appropriate responses.

Math (page 29)
1. C
2. A
3. D
4. B
5. D
6. B
7. C
8. A
9. D
10. B

Math 2 (page 30)
1. A
2. C
3. D
4. B
5. C
6. A
7. D
8. B

Think and Write: September, October, November, December

Answer Key (cont.)

Social Studies (page 31)
1. Central or North America
2. South America
3. Asia
4. Antarctica
5. South America
6. Europe
7. Africa
8. Europe
9. Asia
10. Northern Hemisphere
11. Southern Hemisphere
12. Northern Hemisphere

Social Studies 2 (page 32)
1. west
2. south
3. north
4. east
5. north
6. east
7. south
8. west
9. east
10. north

Science (page 33)
1. D
2. B
3. C
4. A
5. A
6. D
7. C
8. B

Science 2 (page 34)
1. B
2. A
3. D
4. C
5. C
6. A
7. D

Skeleton Analogies (page 35)
1. arm
2. ribs
3. fibula
4. metatarsals
5. patella
6. phalanges
7. tarsals
8. phalanges
Challenge: femur

Spelling (page 36)
1. A
2. B
3. A
4. A
5. C
6. B
7. C
8. B

Homophones (page 37)
Part 1 answers (in any order):
sound alike, not spelled the same, different meanings
1. threw
2. peace
3. sore
4. through
5. soar
6. grown
7. piece
8. groan

Homophones 2 (page 38)
Part 1 answers (in any order):
sound alike, not spelled the same, different meanings
1. flee
2. sew
3. plane
4. sow
5. pier
6. flea
7. plain
8. peer

Challenge:
1. one, won
2. two, too, *or* to
3. four, for
4. eight, ate

The Seven Wonders (page 39)
1. Itaipu
2. England/France
3. Tower
4. North Sea Protection Works
5. Channel Tunnel
6. Golden Gate Bridge
7. Itaipu Dam
8. Panama Canal

Amazing Nines (page 40)
1. A
2. B
3. B
4. B
5. A
6. B

Fun Down Under (page 41)
1. biscuit
2. jillaroo
3. station
4. nappy
5. mate
6. ute
7. outback
8. barbie
9. Accept appropriate responses.
10. Accept appropriate responses.

Review of Analogy Types (page 42)
1. B, plural
2. D, synonym
3. C, adjective
4. A, antonym
5. D, antonym
6. B, synonym
7. A, adjective
8. A, plural
9. C, synonym
10. D, adjective
11. B, antonym
12. C, plural
13. "Pants" is both singular and plural.

Review of Analogy Types 2 (page 43)
1. C, male/female
2. A, purpose
3. D, less than/more than
4. B, homophone
5. A, male/female
6. C, past/present
7. B, member to group
8. B, less than/more than
9. D, present/past (may answer as past/present)
10. A, member to group (may write as group to member)
11. C, homophone
12. D, purpose
13. yes

Use What You Know (page 44)
1. The question words are antonyms. Answers: calf is baby cow (A); synonyms (B); hat is worn on the head (D); A, B and D are not antonyms, so C is correct.
2. B
3. The question words are synonyms. Answers: door is house opening (B); birds fly (C); antonyms (D); B, C, and D are not synonyms, so A must be correct.
4. D

Answer Key (cont.)

Use What You Know 2 (page 45)

1. A fawn is baby deer. Answers: male and female (A); female and male (B); mother and baby (C); Answer must be D. A cygnet is a baby swan.
2. A
3. A herd is group of cattle. Answers: sheep make up flock (B); a puppy is young dog (C); a mare is a female horse (D); Answer must be A. A troop is a group of baboons.
4. C
5. B
6. C
7. A
8. D

Use What You Know 3 (page 46)

1. wrong (all synonyms): A, B, D; correct (antonym): C
2. wrong (all homophones): A, C, D; correct (where found): B
3. wrong (all thing and what it does): A, B, C; correct (synonyms): D

Use What You Know 4 (page 47)

1. wrong (all male to female): A, C, D; correct (what the person does): B
2. C
3. A
4. D
5. B
6. mammal
7. energetic

Analogies in Writing (page 48)

1. A
2. B
3. B
4. A
5. Accept appropriate responses.

Analogies in Writing 2 (page 49)

Accept reasonable responses.

Far Out Analogies (page 50)

Accept appropriate responses.

Analogies in Reading (page 51)

1. B
2. A

Analogies in Reading 2 (page 52)

1. B
2. A

Analogies in Reading 3 (page 53)

1. B
2. A

Connection Review (page 54)

1. J	7. H
2. C	8. B
3. G	9. K
4. A	10. D
5. E	11. I
6. L	12. F

Connection Review 2 (page 55)

1. K	7. I
2. D	8. C
3. H	9. L
4. B	10. E
5. F	11. J
6. A	12. G

Practice Being the Teacher (page 56)

1. approach, near; A: appear, disappear; B: reptile, egg; C: practice, rehearse; D: shrink, grow
2. A and D; antonyms
3. B; synonyms
4. D
5. A and B; should be: present to past, NOT past to present
6. C; learned is not the past tense of students

Practice Being the Teacher 2 (page 57)

1. map to locate; A: donate, give; B: grab, tweezers; C: shame, embarrass; D: screwdriver, turn
2. A and C, synonyms
3. B
4. crocodile : reptile
5. B
6. A and D

Practice What You Know (page 58)

1. B	7. A
2. C	8. B
3. A	9. B
4. D	10. D
5. C	11. A
6. D	12. C

Practice What You Know 2 (page 59)

1. C	7. B
2. D	8. C
3. B	9. C
4. A	10. A
5. D	11. B
6. A	12. D